RAILWAYS OF DERBYSHIRE IN THE TWENTY-FIRST CENTURY

John Jackson

AMBERLEY

First published 2023

Amberley Publishing
The Hill, Stroud
Gloucestershire, GL5 4EP

www.amberley-books.com

Copyright © John Jackson, 2023

The right of John Jackson to be identified as
the Author of this work has been asserted in
accordance with the Copyrights, Designs and
Patents Act 1988.

ISBN 978 1 3981 0267 5 (print)
ISBN 978 1 3981 0268 2 (ebook)

British Library Cataloguing in Publication Data.
A catalogue record for this book is available from
the British Library.

Origination by Amberley Publishing.
Printed in the UK.

Contents

Introduction

My love affair with the county of Derbyshire began over half a century ago. As a teenager, I was both a rail enthusiast and a lover of the great outdoors. For many of those teenage years I was privileged to be a frequent visitor to the county town and railway Mecca of Derby itself. Several years later, and my horizons were widened, and a pair of walking boots purchased. The footwear was primarily for regular visits based close to the Hope Valley railway line and the High Peak village of Edale.

My trusty railway notebook from the spring bank holiday weekend in May 1969 reveals a total of twenty-three diesel locomotives logged together with the various classes of diesel units on display. The Class 40s, 46s and 47s, as well as the pairs of Class 20s, may be long gone, but the line itself has survived. A successful appeal against closure under the Beeching Act led to a late change of plan, which saw this Manchester to Sheffield route via the Hope Valley line reprieved and the route via the Woodhead Tunnel closed instead.

Other railway lines in the county were not so lucky when our railways were rationalised in the 1960s. With the pending electrification of the West Coast Main Line between London Euston and Manchester Piccadilly, the alternative Midland Railway route between Derby, Matlock and Chinley was perceived as an expensive duplication. After several years of delay, the line was eventually closed through much of Derbyshire, between Matlock and Chinley, and main line services diverted along the longer route via Chesterfield and the Hope Valley.

This was probably the most high-profile line closure in the county following the Beeching Report's recommendations. It may yet, however, see reinstatement as today's government once again considers potential candidates for reopening.

Take a glance at the county's rail map today and the fragmentation of its passenger lines is clear. For instance, making a rail journey between the towns of Matlock and Buxton, a distance of just over twenty road miles via the A6, involves travelling around the perimeter of the county and the unlikely use of at least four different trains. Closer study of the rail map also shows just what an impact the Pennine Hills have had in shaping the county's transport links. Often referred to as the Backbone of England, the county of Derbyshire sits astride the southern end of these formidable moorlands. The rail pioneers faced a daunting challenge when attempting to combat these hills when railway construction was in its heyday.

Despite the loss of its main London to Manchester artery, the county of Derbyshire retains a rather fragmented rail network. Although around one hundred of the county's stations may have been closed during the twentieth century, almost forty have survived and continue to serve the county's population of around 800,000. In this publication we take a look at those lines and stations that have survived into the twenty-first century. A map showing the county's surviving passenger rail lines appears at the start of the photos section. Some additional lines, particularly in the Buxton and Peak Forest area, are currently used only by freight services.

Several of the country's passenger operators provide services both within and through the county of Derbyshire. Arriva CrossCountry services connect the North East of England and Scotland with Birmingham and the South West, as well as providing Derby with a service linking Nottingham, Birmingham and Cardiff. East Midlands Railway operate the key route between Sheffield and London St Pancras via Chesterfield and Derby. They also provide a number of secondary services within the county. To the north of the county, Northern Rail and First TransPennine Express operate services along the Hope Valley and to and from Buxton.

In common with much of the UK, the county has seen a major shift in the type of freight traffic conveyed on its railway lines. Sitting in the heart of the Yorkshire, Nottinghamshire and Derbyshire coalfield, the commercial extraction of coal and subsequent movement to power station dominated the freight traffic in the county. At one stage there were nearly seventy collieries in the county. By the mid-1990s coal mining in the county was a thing of the past. The area does, however, remain rich in other valuable materials found below its surface. The importance of this large-scale commercial quarrying to the region's railways is evident throughout the pages of this publication. We take a closer look at the freight-only lines in the Peak Forest area, near Buxton, together with the freight movements to and from Earles Sidings in the Hope Valley.

The county's north to south rail arteries also witness a variety of other freight traffic passing through its borders including regular workings of both intermodal container and steel trains.

Once an important part of the rail industry's coal hub, the extensive yards and maintenance depot at Toton, on the county's border with Nottinghamshire, remain in use today. The depot is the main operations hub of the country's biggest freight operator, DB Cargo. In addition, the yard and depot see visitors of all the major freight operators' locomotives.

As well as the major rail complex at Toton, the former steam roundhouse at Barrow Hill, to the north-east of the town of Chesterfield, is another survivor from the nineteenth century. Closed by British Rail in 1991, the general rundown of the structure was eventually halted and then reversed and it remains as the country's last working roundhouse to this day. As well as being home to a variety of motive power, this rail hub prides itself in being a centre for learning and work experience for all ages.

While this book focuses on the railways that have survived as part of the national network, there are also several preserved railways within the county. Three of these are particularly worthy of mention. We therefore take a brief look at the operations of Ecclesbourne Valley Railway, Peak Rail and the Midland Railway Trust.

Finally, as a regular traveller across the county, I feel qualified to compliment the efforts of Derbyshire County Council in their initiatives in providing integrated public transport for the county's visitors. In particular it is my frequent use of their attractively priced Derbyshire Wayfarer ticket that has resulted in my obtaining many of the photos gathered here. The countywide ticket is valid on rail services after 09.00 on Monday to Friday and at any time on Saturdays, Sundays and bank holidays. This validity extends to all four of the county's passenger operators outlined above. The integrated travel opportunities of this ticket are demonstrated by its acceptance on virtually all bus operators' services within the county.

Our journey around the county's railway scene commences in the city of Derby and the subsequent chapters follow a broadly clockwise journey around the county starting in its south-west corner.

I hope you enjoy your journey through the pages of this book as much as I have enjoyed compiling them.

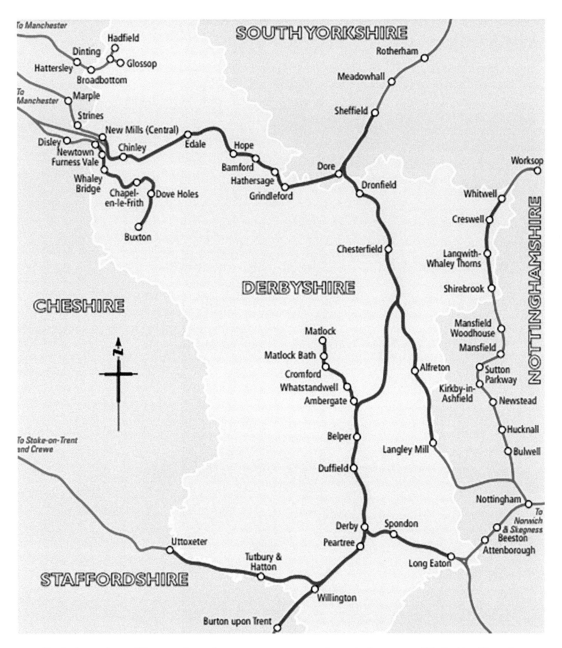

Derbyshire rail map. This map shows the surviving passenger railways in the county of Derbyshire. Since the map's production, the station at Ilkeston has reopened.

Derby

We commence our journey around Derbyshire with the city of Derby itself. The city has a long railway history with the locomotive sheds, workshops and several stations making the industry an important employer in the area. Today, Derby is served by one main station on the south-eastern edge of the city centre. It is now known simply as Derby, although the frontage still carries the former name of Derby Midland, as seen in this photo taken in April 2017.

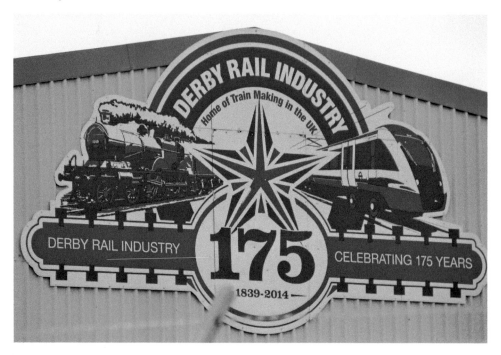

Derby's railway workshops date back to 1839. This sign, at the Litchurch Lane works, commemorates the industry's 175th anniversary in the city in 2014.

Throughout its history, Derby has enjoyed a fast and frequent passenger service to London's St Pancras station. Today, East Midlands Railway (EMR) operate a half-hourly service on the Sheffield to London corridor. On 27 November 2018, seven-car Meridian unit, No. 222002 *The Cutler's Company*, is seen awaiting departure on the 13.02 service to London.

Derby station is also an important calling point for Arriva CrossCountry services on the north-east to south-west corridor, centred on Birmingham New Street. On 5 December 2017, their five-car Voyager unit, No. 221124, arrives at platform 1, forming the 10.44 service to Edinburgh Waverley.

The regular Voyager workings on this route are complemented by CrossCountry's small fleet of High Speed Train sets. On 8 March 2018, power car No. 43207 leads a southbound rake into Derby station on a service to Plymouth.

These long-distance CrossCountry services are complemented by Class 170 diesel multiple units linking the cities of Birmingham and Nottingham, involving reversal in Derby station. On 31 March 2017, two-car unit No. 170518 is seen on an eastbound service towards Nottingham.

East Midlands Railway (EMR) also operate local services in the Derby area. On 16 February 2018, No. 158806 waits in Derby's platform 2b to form the 10.42 service to Crewe.

These hourly Derby to Crewe services are normally operated by single coach Class 153 units, sometimes in pairs. On 28 February 2017, No. 153308 is about to terminate at Derby on a morning arrival from Crewe.

EMR also operate an hourly service linking Matlock with Nottingham and Newark. On 27 November 2018, No. 156415 waits for departure on the 12.52 service to Matlock.

The routine handling of the two passenger operators' services was enhanced by remodelling the station area in 2018. This included the removal of the existing bay platform 5 and replacing it with a new island platform numbered 6 and 7. This view shows the construction work on 22 June that year, with EMR's four-car Meridian, No. 222103, on the left.

Derby is also the base for Network Rail test trains. The locomotives and stock involved occupy part of the former Railway Technical Centre (RTC) area adjacent to the running lines towards Long Eaton and Nottingham. This view, taken on 31 March 2017, shows a variety of locomotives and rolling stock stabled in the RTC area. The Long Eaton lines are in the centre of picture and EMR's stabling point at Etches Park lies away to the left.

In this RTC view, Network Rail's familiar yellow livery dominates the scene. On 20 June 2018, diesel shunter No. 08417 continues to see use in the local area. It was built back in 1958 and has been based at Derby throughout this century.

A few months earlier, the area was still home to long withdrawn sister loco, No. 08536. The former No. D3700, built at BR Works at Darlington in 1959 and still retaining its blue era livery, had been stored here since 1995.

Two more veteran machines were on view in the RTC area on 15 November 2016. Class 08 shunter No. 08762 is owned by RMS Locotec and has since been reported at Great Yarmouth, while Class 31 No. 31105 is now preserved at the Mangapps Railway Museum in Essex.

The RTC area is occupied by Network Rail and Loram UK Ltd. Loram specialises in maintaining rolling stock and permanent way vehicles. On 10 March 2017, former Class 73 loco No. 73139, now unnumbered, is seen in its new guise as a static advertisement for Loram's services.

More unusual Network Rail locomotive power was provided for their test train marshalling on 11 January 2019. London Transport-liveried No. 20142 is seen on a reversing move in Derby station with an unidentified diesel shunter on the rear.

On 19 January 2017, more familiar motive power was provided by Direct Rail Services (DRS) to accompany Network Rail's inspection saloon, affectionally named Caroline. The saloon requires electric train heating, usually provided by one of DRS' fleet of Class 37s. On this date, loco No. 37405 was their power choice.

Colas Rail also regularly supply motive power for Network Rail test trains. On 28 June 2017, Colas' pair of Class 67s, No. 67023 *Stella* and No. 67027 *Charlotte*, are seen operating in top-and-tail mode while reversing alongside Derby station. The following year these tracks were to be removed to make room for the new island platform.

Derby's Litchurch Lane works have a long association with the building of new rolling stock. It has been the UK's sole surviving manufacturer since Alstom's Washwood Heath plant in Birmingham closed in 2005. In this typical perimeter view, the works yard is home to shunters Nos 08602 and 08682, together with several newly constructed Class 710 carriages for London Overground.

These Class 710 'Aventra' units are being built by Bombardier Transportation for London Overground. Forty-five units are being constructed. On a snowy day in March 2018, an unnumbered driving car is seen in the works yard.

Another important rolling stock order will see over 400 carriages of Class 720 electric units delivered by Bombardier for Abellio Greater Anglia, as part of that company's fleet replacement programme. One of these units is seen in the works yard on 31 March 2019.

Another major customer of Bombardier Transportation is London Underground (LUL), with Derby station seeing movement of completed sets between the Litchurch Lane workshops and transfer onto LUL lines at Ruislip in West London. On 19 March 2014, a reversal in the station area sees Nos 20107 and 20096 nearest the camera, before the cavalcade heads south.

Bombardier have also produced the Class 345 units in readiness for the much publicised and heavily delayed Crossrail project. On 20 September 2017, No. 345017 is waiting to depart the station area. It is being hauled by No. 67006 and bound for the test track at Old Dalby, north of Melton Mowbray.

The Class 44, 45 and 46 'Peak' diesels have a long association with Derby. The fifty-six members of Class 46 were built at the works here in the early 1960s and were regular performers in the area until all were withdrawn by the mid-1980s. Fortunately No. 46045, seen here on 8 September 2016 and carrying its pre-TOPS number of D182, survived into preservation. The loco is currently based at the Midland Railway, Butterley.

There was more heritage traction in the area on 9 November 2015, with two locos both carrying the Northern Belle livery, No. 47790 *Galloway Princess* and No. 57312 *Solway Princess*. The pair were about to leave on a light engine move back to Crewe Gresty Bridge depot.

On 7 January 2016, it's the turn of a pair of Colas Rail Class 56 locos to be stabled. With No. 56087 for company, No. 56302 is seen alongside the station platform while waiting its next turn of duty.

Many of the light engine moves in the Derby area involve Direct Rail Services' depot at Crewe. On 21 July 2016, a four-loco convoy arrives on a move from Crewe to Barrow Hill, near Chesterfield. A pair of Class 37s, Nos 37606 and 37612, are in the company of a pair of Class 68s, No. 68005 *Defiant* and No. 68022 *Resolution*. Half a century separates these two loco classes, with the Class 37s being built in 1963 and the Class 68s in 2014.

Just about any type of loco can make an appearance through Derby. On 13 November 2014, however, this convoy involved No. 59003 *Yeoman Highlander* being moved by Nos 20311 and 20314 from Immingham Docks to Eastleigh. The loco had been acquired by GB Railfreight. It had just returned to the UK after spending thirteen years working in Germany.

Most freight traffic is routed away from Derby station using the freight only lines through nearby Toton Yard. The virtual elimination of coal traffic in recent years has seen Derby's freight numbers reduce still further. Before the coal cessation, Freightliner Heavy Haul's No. 66512 heads south through the station on 21 March 2014. The imported coal is being taken from Immingham Docks to the now closed power station at Rugeley in Staffordshire.

One freight working, operated by DB Cargo, has been a mainstay through Derby for many years. The northbound empty steel wagons are being returned from Wolverhampton Steel Terminal to Immingham on 29 March 2018. A regular Class 60 working, on this occasion No. 60007 *The Spirit of Tom Kendell* was in charge.

South-west Derbyshire Survivors – Willington, Peartree and Tutbury & Hatton

Several local stations in south-west Derbyshire have survived into the twenty-first century. These include the station at Peartree, on the outskirts of Derby itself. It is served on weekdays by just two trains in each direction, between Derby and Crewe. On 31 July 2019, single coach unit No. 153384 calls on a Derby-bound service.

The station at Willington sees the majority of services passing through without stopping. On 22 June 2018, Voyager No. 221123 speeds through on a long-distance CrossCountry service.

A few minutes later, two-car unit No. 170521 makes a call at Willington on a Nottingham-bound service. Repton & Willington station was closed in 1964, but the new station, simply called Willington, opened in the 1990s and is served by eight trains a day in each direction on the Derby to Burton upon Trent line.

The original station called Tutbury (in Staffordshire) was closed to passengers in 1966. A new station, called Tutbury and Hatton, was opened in 1989. Both the village of Hatton and the station itself lie just inside Derbyshire, around 12 miles from Derby. The staggered platforms straddle the level crossing and the signal box, together with its local semaphore signals, remains manned.

On 22 June 2018, single car units were seen on these Derby to Stoke on Trent and Crewe services. First, No. 153357 calls on a service heading for Crewe.

Secondly, No 153311 approaches the platform on an East Midlands Railway service from Crewe to Derby. The station currently enjoys an hourly service in both directions, including Sunday afternoons.

Derby to Matlock

This 17-mile branch line retains a passenger service, with Duffield station the first calling point on leaving Derby. On 22 March 2018, a pair of Class 153 units, Nos 153311 and 153313, call on a northbound service to Matlock.

On 24 October 2020, two-car unit No. 156470 is working this branch service also bound for Matlock. The Duffield platform on the right is on the former branch to Wirksworth, now used by private operator Ecclesbourne Valley Railway.

7 miles to the north of Derby lies the town of Belper. Despite the town's population being in excess of 20,000, no CrossCountry services call here. On 24 October 2020, a pair of Voyagers, Nos 220024 and 221141, pass on a southbound service.

Almost all of EMR's Meridian services also pass without stopping, such as 222007 seen here on a southbound service the same day. Just one working to and from Sheffield calls here on weekdays, timed so as at provide a service for those that work in the Yorkshire city.

By the time the station at Ambergate is reached, the main Derby to Sheffield line has been left behind. Just a single track remains on the branch between here and Matlock. EMR unit No. 156916, in the company's revised livery, is seen arriving at the curved platform on a Matlock service.

The next stop on the Matlock branch is at Whatstandwell. On 22 March 2018, No. 156413 is seen arriving on a service to Matlock.

The next station is at Cromford, where the station buildings survive and are Grade II listed. On 24 October 2020, No. 156497 calls at the former northbound platform, with the building on the abandoned platform opposite now in private ownership. The unit will shortly enter the 700-metre-long Willersley Tunnel as it heads towards Matlock.

These hourly branch services have been handled by Class 153 and 156 units for many years. On 21 July 2016, this view of Matlock Bath station shows unit No. 156413 making its call.

Journey's end on the branch line nowadays is at Matlock, with EMT services using the former southbound platform. On 21 July 2016, a pair of Class 153 units, Nos 153374 and 153357, are waiting to depart. The opposite platform is in the hands of Peak Rail and used for services northwards along the route of the now closed Midland Railway route to Manchester Central.

Later the same day it is the turn of No. 156405 on a branch line service. Since 2015, these weekday services have operated through to Newark Castle, via the Derby and Nottingham corridor.

EMR's Class 158s also make occasional appearances at Matlock on these services. On 31 October 2015, No. 158864 is about to return on a service to Nottingham. Through rail services to the north of Matlock ceased back in June 1968.

The closed line between Derby and Ripley left the main Sheffield line just south of Duffield, via a junction near the village of Little Eaton. It survived into the twenty-first century, providing rail access to Denby Coal Disposal Point. In this view, Class 58 loco No. 58025 is seen making slow progress, negotiating one of the many level crossings on the branch. The ending of this traffic led to the junction's connection to the main line being removed in 2002. The rails on the branch were eventually lifted a decade later.

Ecclesbourne Valley Railway (EVR)

This book focuses on Derbyshire's lines that form part of the national rail network. Several preserved lines and locations in the county are, however, worthy of mention, including the EVR. The company operate services on the former Wirksworth branch, which left the main line at Duffield. A two-car unit, Nos 53599 and 51360, calls at the intermediate station at Idridgehay.

The EVR's owners, WyvernRail, secured the transfer of the line from Network Rail in 2015. Services are operated northwards to Ravenstor, about half a mile from the company's base at Wirksworth, which is reached via a 1 in 30 steep incline. In this view, single car railbus M79900 is seen at the platform at Ravenstor.

The yard at Wirksworth is home to a variety of rolling stock. In this view, a number of the company's first generation diesel multiple unit cars are on display.

In September 2013, Wirksworth yard was home to several preserved locomotives, including Brush Type 2 loco No. D5814.

On the same day, BRCW Type 3 loco No. 33035 was also resident in the yard. This is a well-travelled locomotive since entering preservation and is currently at the Wensleydale Railway in North Yorkshire.

The line is also home to a pair of former Gatwick Express Luggage Vans. One of these, No. 9101, was in use as a static museum at Wirksworth at the time of this 2013 visit.

Peak Rail

The closure of the London St Pancras to Manchester Central through route, via Matlock and Bakewell, in the late 1960s meant the loss of passenger services for a number of communities in the county. Around twenty years later, the line between Matlock and Rowsley was acquired by preservation company, Peak Rail. They have restored the station at Darley Dale, which was derelict but, thankfully, the period buildings had not been demolished. This was the view looking north from the level crossing on Station Road on 22 March 2018.

On the same day, this is the view to the south of Darley Dale crossing. On the Up side of the line a number of locos are stabled. These include Dutch Railways shunter No. 685 in the foreground.

The site of the former BR depot at Rowsley is now home to Peak Rail's Rowsley South station, about a mile from the original BR station, which lies to the north. Today. this substantial site is the main base of the company's activities. On 31 March 2019, former NCB steam loco No. 7 is seen at the site.

The Peak classes of diesel locomotive have a long association with the county of Derbyshire. It is appropriate, therefore, for Peak Rail to be home to one of the first ten Class 44 locos, built at Derby Works at the end of the 1950s. On the same day in March 2019, No. 44008, carrying its original number D8 and its name *Penyghent*, is seen moving in the yard.

Further north, almost 10 miles of the former BR trackbed now forms the Monsal Trail. This is a dedicated traffic-free route for walkers and cyclists. The terrain inevitably includes both tunnels and viaducts, including the spectacular Headstone viaduct. This view, taken on 3 April 2019, emulates the one used in early British Railways posters in an attempt to lure travellers to the Peak District area.

The village of Millers Dale once boasted an extensive station and was the junction for the connecting local service to Buxton. Today the long-closed station provides services for users of the Monsal Trail. While there has long been a campaign to reinstate the railway line between Matlock and Millers Dale, there are many users of the trail who feel equally strongly that any such move would disadvantage them if the trail were removed. As will be seen later in this publication, the operators of the quarries further north are important customers of the rail industry. They would undoubtedly benefit from a quicker route to their markets further south.

Buxton towards Manchester

Closure of the line to Millers Dale and the south half a century ago left Buxton as the terminus of a 25-mile line to Manchester. On 1 April 2019, No. 150223 waits while forming an early evening service to Manchester Piccadilly.

These services are operated by Northern, using their fleet of Class 150 and Class 156 two-car units. On 18 October 2020, No. 150147 is stabled awaiting its next duties.

On the morning of 21 March 2018, it is the turn of No. 156481 to be working on the Buxton line. It is seen at the terminus about to leave on the 09.27 departure to Manchester Piccadilly.

Two stations were originally built by rival companies to serve Buxton, with the local planners insisting they were built side by side. The former Midland Railway station served the line towards Rowsley and was demolished. The surviving London & North Western Railway (LNWR) station survives providing the service to Manchester. The remains of a recent snowfall are evident in this scene showing the LNWR station on 20 March 2018. A four-car formation, consisting of Nos 150118 and 156440, is seen in platform 1.

The first station on the line towards Manchester is at the village of Dove Holes. The important quarry here is covered in the Peak Forest section of this book. The line through the station here is used solely for the Buxton to Manchester passenger service. On 22 October 2020, No. 150136 departs on a service to Manchester Piccadilly.

On the same day, sister unit No. 150110 is seen heading in the opposite direction, slowing to call on a service to Buxton. There are limited facilities for the handful of passengers using this unmanned station each day. There are no period buildings and just two small, modern bus shelter-style waiting rooms.

The next stop is the town of Chapel-en-le-Frith, where the station is located around a mile from, and sits above, the town centre. Although unstaffed, the station building has survived and is on the left in this view, looking towards Buxton.

In common with many secondary lines in Derbyshire, the area retains its semaphore signalling and associated signal boxes. On 2 April 2019, No. 150112 passes Chapel-en-le-Frith box with a Manchester-bound service. An earlier box, on the opposite side of the tracks, was demolished in a freight train accident in 1957. The driver of a runaway train, John Axon, was posthumously awarded the George Cross. Electric loco No. 86261 was named in his honour in 1981.

The town of Whaley Bridge is the next calling point, and this was the view of the station on 2 April 2019, looking in the direction of Buxton, just over 9 miles away.

On that day a pair of Class 150 units, Nos 150122 and 150110, make a call at Whaley Bridge on a service to Buxton.

The village of Furness Vale, a mile to the north of Whaley Bridge, retains its passenger services. On 2 April 2019, No. 150211 calls to pick up a couple of customers for this Manchester Piccadilly service.

The next station on the line is New Mills Newtown. This station lies close to the county borders of Derbyshire and Cheshire, hence its inclusion here. It also serves as an interchange with New Mills Central station, which is served by Hope Valley line services. The connection is not particularly convenient, however, as it involves a fifteen-minute walk across the valley. On 2 April 2019, two-car unit No. 150210 calls at Newtown on a Buxton service. These services continue beyond here towards Stockport and Manchester.

Peak Forest

In common with the other intermediate stations along the line, Peak Forest station closed to passengers in March 1967. The northbound station buildings remain intact and were subsequently used as a BR staff signing on point.

Since privatisation, these buildings have been used as office accommodation for EWS, now DB Cargo UK. Two of their Class 66 locos, Nos 66051 and 66021, can be seen stabled in the background in this photo. The site is close to the community of Peak Dale.

It is the area's two rail-served quarries that keep Peak Forest firmly on the railway map today. Tarmac's Tunstead and Cemex's Dove Holes limestone quarries account for the movement of several million tons by rail annually. On 22 March 2015, No. 66104 stands in Dove Holes quarry while its rake of wagons is loaded.

On 21 October 2019, DB Cargo's No. 60044 *Dowlow* has just emerged from the 3,000-yard-long Dove Holes Tunnel and passes the quarry of the same name with a rake of empty hoppers from Warrington Arpley to Tunstead.

GB Railfreight also operate an increasing number of services to and from Peak Forest. On 19 October 2019, No. 66737 *Lesia* pulls a rake of box wagons out of Dove Holes Quarry. It will run round its train in the sidings at Peak Forest before its departure.

In 2019, GB Railfreight used a pair of Class 56 locomotives for shunting duties in the Peak Forest area. On 31 March 2019, No. 56081 is stabled between duties.

Meanwhile, classmate No. 56098 is in shunting action a few days later. It is seen here in Dove Holes quarry while the GB train is loaded.

Direct Rail Services' (DRS) Class 66 locomotives are rarely seen in the Peak Forest area. In Autumn 2020, however, GB Railfreight hired a DRS loco to assist with their shunting at the quarry. On 19 October, No. 66433 is about to move on to the quarry sidings.

DB Cargo locomotives dominate this Peak Forest scene on 20 March 2018. A pair of Class 66 locos, Nos 66137 and 66019, are in the fuel point with No. 66030 in the yard beyond on the right. Meanwhile, No. 66051 is about to pass Peak Forest signal box. Semaphore signals prevail in this area and this box, by far the largest in the area, has around fifty levers.

DB Cargo light engine moves between the stabling point at Peak Forest and the company's Toton base are commonplace. This on 20 October 2020, however, was a little unusual. Royal-liveried Class 67 No. 67005 *Queen's Messenger* had been waiting a move back to Toton for attention. It is seen here about to depart as a light engine convoy, sandwiched in between Nos 66082 and 66069.

In a busy scene at Dove Holes on 21 March 2018, three DB Cargo Class 66 locomotives are waiting for loading to be completed before each pulling out of the quarry. With No. 66088 in the background, Nos 66137 and 66019 are in the foreground.

Freightliner has recently renewed its long-term contract with Tarmac at Tunstead, requiring several of its locos to be outbased at the quarry. This also necessitates light engine moves to and from either their stabling point at Earles Sidings, Hope Valley, or their main depot at Leeds Balm Road. On 20 March 2018, a three-loco convoy passes Dove Holes while working from Tunstead to Leeds. The convoy contains Nos 66622, 66606 and 66602, on the rear.

On 21 October 2020, GB Railfreight's No. 66785 is seen approaching Great Rocks Junction with empty wagons from Small Heath to Tunstead. The sidings at Peak Forest are in the background.

Class 60 loco No. 60044 has deposited its rake of wagons in Tunstead and has just been given the signal by Great Rocks Junction signal box to run light engine back to Peak Forest for stabling.

The signal box at Great Rocks Junction controls the lines to and from Peak Forest and the entrance to Tunstead works. In addition, it controls the single line section between here and Buxton via Topley Pike.

This is the view of Tunstead, with Great Rocks Junction signal box to the right of the photo. The left-hand track is the single line through to Buxton, while the right-hand line is used for locos and trains to and from Tunstead. On 2 April 2019, No. 66607 waits for the signal before reversing into Tunstead loco stabling area. Sister locos No. 66619 *Derek W. Johnson MBE* and No. 66622 are already stabled.

The former Buxton to Ashbourne line remains in use as far as the quarries at Hindlow and Dowlow. On 23 October 2020, No. 66140 is seen in Briggs Sidings, Dowlow, waiting to leave on a working to Ashburys in Manchester.

This train will first take the 5-mile, single line section to Buxton where the loco will run round its train in the recently extended Up Reception Sidings. It is seen passing the village of Harpur Hill within this single-track section.

After running round, the train then operates via Ashwood Dale and Pic Tor Tunnels, offering few, if any, photo opportunities. The working then emerges passing Tunstead and Great Rocks Junction. Three days earlier, the same working is seen approaching Great Rocks Junction signal box. The driver is handing the section's single-track token to the signalman. The loco that day was No. 66115.

The train then passes Peak Forest, where No. 66140 is seen again about to finally make its escape from the area! It will shortly enter Dove Holes Tunnel and then join the Sheffield to Manchester line via the triangular junction just east of Chinley. This junction is in the hamlet of Chapel Milton, which gives its name to the two-forked viaduct at this location.

Glossop, Dinting and Hadfield

In the north-west corner of the county lies a surviving section of the former route between Manchester and Sheffield via Penistone. The Woodhead route through the Pennines was closed completely by the early 1980s, despite the Beeching Report recommending retention of this Woodhead route and closing the route via the Hope Valley instead. The latter line is covered in the next section of this book. On 2 April 2019, Northern electric unit No. 323233 arrives at the single platform terminus at Glossop.

Immediately adjacent to the station at Dinting is the viaduct of the same name. Northern unit No. 323233 is seen again in this view as it crosses the impressive structure.

On 2 April 2019, sister unit No. 323228 is waiting to leave Hadfield on a service to Manchester Piccadilly. Although in Derbyshire and served by Northern, these three stations are included in the Transport for Greater Manchester (TfGM) area operationally, although not benefiting from TfGM concessionary fares.

This is the view from Hadfield station platform looking in the opposite direction. Beyond the buffer stops, the line east of here towards Crowden was closed to passengers in 1970, and completely in the early 1980s. The 16-mile trackbed between here and the South Yorkshire town of Penistone, via the infamous Woodhead Tunnel, now forms part of the Trans Pennine Trail.

The Hope Valley – New Mills Central to Grindleford

As already mentioned, this Manchester to Sheffield passenger route was retained after a last-minute reversal and the through route via Woodhead Tunnel closed instead. These Hope Valley stopping services call at New Mills Central station, operated by Northern. This is the view from platform 1, looking towards Manchester. The original station buildings remain, to the left of the photo.

The village of Chinley once boasted an important junction station between Sheffield, Manchester, Derby and London St Pancras. Today its importance is much reduced, served via an island platform enabling stopping services from Sheffield to Manchester to call. Northern's new fleet of Class 195 units have started appearing on these local services. On 22 October 2020, No. 195011 calls on a service to Sheffield.

The hourly EMR services from Norwich to Liverpool, via Nottingham and Manchester, pass non-stop through Chinley. On 21 March 2018, No. 158780 leads No. 158847 on a service to Liverpool Lime Street.

Chinley station also sees freight traffic from the Peak Forest area quarries bound for the Manchester area. This traffic includes the Dowlow to Ashburys working featured earlier in this book. On the same day No. 60015 heads west through Chinley on this service to Ashburys, Manchester.

The Peak Forest line veers southwards at the triangular junction to the east of Chinley. The Hope Valley line continues eastwards towards Sheffield and enters the 3,700-yard-long Cowburn Tunnel shortly afterwards. On 20 October 2020, Freightliner's No. 66620 has just emerged from the tunnel's eastern portal and is passing through Edale station on a working from Tunstead to Radlett, in Hertfordshire.

Heading in the opposite direction through Edale station on 1 April 2019 is GB Railfreight's No. 66788. It is returning to Peak Forest with a rake of empty hoppers from Washwood Heath in Birmingham.

A rare Sunday freight train movement, on 22 March 2015, sees DB Cargo's No. 60092 heading west through Edale. It is returning a rake of empty wagons from Attercliffe Sidings in Sheffield to Peak Forest.

The Hope Valley line sees a variety of light engine movements in order to service Derbyshire's freight customers. On 1 April 2019, No. 66757 *West Somerset Railway* passes Edale on a Peak Forest to Doncaster Roberts Road depot move.

Freightliner light engine loco moves are also common along the Hope Valley, particular between the stabling points at Earles Sidings, between Edale and Hope, and Tunstead. On 3 April 2019, No. 66605 heads west through Edale-bound for Tunstead.

Northern has recently stopped using the Class 142 Pacer units. On 21 March 2018, No. 142048 calls at Edale on a stopping service to Sheffield. It is passed by First TransPennine Express (FTPE) Class 185 unit No. 185144, heading for Manchester with a service from Cleethorpes. Most of these FTPE services operate non-stop from Sheffield to Stockport.

Prior to the introduction of their Class 185 units, these FPTE services were in the hands of Class 170 units. On 22 March 2015, No. 170307 leads a sister two-car unit on a service to Cleethorpes. The service is seen passing Edale signal box.

Northern's fleet of units includes new Class 195s, operating right across their franchise area. Their introduction has enabled the Pacers to be withdrawn. On 21 October 2020, No. 195024 is seen between Edale and Hope.

This long-standing freight flow from Peak Forest to Bletchley dates back to the days of British Rail. Following rail privatisation in the 1990s, it was then operated by DB Cargo for over twenty years. On 21 March 2018, No. 66051 is seen between Hope and Edale working the return empty hoppers.

Two years later, on 21 October 2020, the same working, photographed in roughly the same location, is in the hands of freight operator GB Railfreight, with No. 66770 in charge.

Hope Cement Works was opened by the Earle family around 100 years ago and, after several changes of ownership, has been owned by the Breedon Group since 2016. It is the largest cement works in the UK. Throughout this period, the works have remained connected to the main rail network via a series of exchange sidings around 2 miles away. This was the view of the sidings on 2 April 2019, with No. 66622 stabled.

This is the wintry scene at the aptly named Earles Sidings on 20 March 2018 looking east towards Sheffield, with the cement works out of view on the right. The rake of HTA wagons is used for delivery of coal to the cement kilns. Locos Nos 66614 and 66587 are stabled behind.

Freightliner have a small fleet of Class 66 locos outbased in Derbyshire, for traffic operating to and from Earles Sidings and Tunstead. These are predominantly Class 66/6 locos, with occasional Class 66/5 and Class 70 locos making an appearance. On 20 October 2020, Nos 66617 and 70015 are awaiting their next duties.

The extensive fleet of wagons used by Hope Cement Works includes a number of short-wheel-based PCA type cement wagons built in the 1980s. Earlier on 20 October 2020, No. 66617 nears its journey's end working a rake of these empty wagons following unloading at Dewsbury, West Yorkshire. The loco is passing through Hope station and will shortly deposit them in Earles Sidings. The works' own fleet of diesel shunters will then trip them to the works when required.

Hope station is unmanned and situated east of the village itself. It also serves as a railhead for the nearby tourist centre of Castleton. On the same day, a pair of FTPE Class 185s, No. 185137 on the rear with No. 185117 leading, pass through Hope on a service to Cleethorpes.

The village station at Bamford is 2 miles to the east of Hope. Northern's Pacers may have disappeared but their fleet of Class 150s, built in the mid-1980s, remain in service on local routes. On 2 April 2019, No. 150127, built in 1986, arrives at Bamford on a stopping service to Sheffield.

Most East Midlands Railway services between Nottingham and Liverpool are worked by pairs of Class 158 units. Their Class 156s do, however, make less frequent appearances, such as No. 156406 seen here passing Bamford on 21 March 2018, with No. 158774 for company on the rear.

The village station at Hathersage, 11 miles west of Sheffield, is the next stop on these Northern services. On 21 March 2018, No. 150269 slows to call on a service to Sheffield.

On the same day, Freightliner Class 66 No. 66587 heads west through Hathersage station. It is working the returning empty cement wagons from Dewsbury to Earles Sidings.

The final Derbyshire station on the Hope Valley line is at Grindleford. On 21 March 2018, No. 66518 heads east through the station on a cement working from Earles Sidings to West Burton Power Station in Nottinghamshire.

Barrow Hill, Staveley

The village of Barrow Hill lies about 5 miles north of Chesterfield. It was a British Railways steam shed until 1965. It was allocated the depot code 41E within the Eastern Region during the later steam days and then BH during its diesel era. On complete closure by British Rail in 1991 it fell into disrepair. The Grade II listed building has since been given a new lease of life and is one of the country's best railway museums and heritage centres. This view shows just some of the various classes of locos gathered at the depot on 10 November 2013.

The Barrow Hill roundhouse, with the turntable as its centrepiece, is home to a mix of preserved steam, diesel and electric locomotives. On 21 November 2018, diesel shunter No. 03066 was stabled on the turntable. This shunter originally carried the number D2066 when built in 1959.

On the same day, the roundhouse also housed shunter No. 02003. Built a year later, in 1960, it carried the number D2853 in its BR days.

A much older occupant of the roundhouse is former BR 0-6-0 tank engine No. 41708, which was built in 1880. Its survival in preservation in this Derbyshire community is particularly appropriate as the loco was based at Staveley Ironworks for its last twenty years' working life, until withdrawal in 1965.

Another steam locomotive occupying the roundhouse in 2018 was Midland Compound No. 1000. This Midland Railway 4-4-0 loco was built at Derby in 1902.

The extensive Barrow Hill site is also home to a variety of locos in the yard area outside, complete with a viewing platform. This line up shows No. 20301 nearest the camera, then Nos 20304, 20309, 20308, 20312, 89001 and 37421.

On 21 October 2018, the yard was home to No. 27066. It was built by Birmingham Railway Carriage & Wagon Company, as No. D5386, in 1962. After a few years working from depots on the Midland Main Line, it spent most of its working life in Scotland. It was withdrawn from BR service as long ago as 1987.

In 2013, Barrow Hill yard was home to dilapidated Class 37 No. 37503. This English Electric Type 3 loco was built in 1961 as D6717. The former EWS-liveried machine was undergoing repair work at the Wensleydale Railway before being interrupted by the Covid-19 pandemic.

Also present the same day was English Electric Type 4 loco, No. 40012. The Class 40 had been returned to the BR green livery it carried when built in 1959. It also sports its original name Aureol.

Midland Main Line Class 45 'Peak' loco No. 45060 was built at Crewe in 1961 as No. D100. It is seen here in Barrow Hill yard in 2018, still carrying its Sherwood Forester nameplates.

Several elderly electric locos are also resident at Barrow Hill. These include No. E5001, built for the Southern Region of British Railways in 1958. The Bo-Bo Class 71 electric was withdrawn as long ago as 1977.

Another veteran electric machine is No. 82008, which has been at Barrow Hill since the turn of the century. Built in 1961 as E3054, the loco is owned by AC Locomotive Group, and now sports InterCity livery.

Chesterfield

The town of Chesterfield is Derbyshire's second largest, behind Derby itself, with a population in excess of 100,000 people. Its railway station is strategically placed on the network with lines to both Derby and Nottingham to the south and Sheffield to the north. The town enjoys two trains an hour to and from London St Pancras throughout the day. One of these is a fast service calling only at Derby and Leicester, operated by the East Midlands Railways (EMR) fleet of seven-car Meridians. On 5 June 2015, No. 222003 *Tornado* calls on a service from London to Sheffield.

The semi-fast services to and from St Pancras are usually formed of EMR five-car Meridians. On 16 February 2018, No. 222008 *Derby Etches Park* is calling on a London-bound service. A northbound CrossCountry Trains' Voyager, No. 221127, is seen in the adjacent platform.

CrossCountry Trains operates passenger services on the north-east to south-west axis through Birmingham. On 7 August 2019, four-car unit No. 220026 is seen departing on a service to Plymouth.

EMR High Speed Trains had largely been displaced on their services through Chesterfield by the time this photo was taken. On 7 August 2019, former Grand Central power cars, with No. 43468 leading, depart Chesterfield on 14.13 to London St Pancras.

EMR's services from Liverpool to Norwich also call here hourly in both directions, with services to and from Liverpool reversing at Sheffield station. On 29 January 2019, No. 158806 leads No. 158846 on a service to Liverpool Lime Street.

Northern is the third passenger train operator serving Chesterfield, with their hourly service linking Nottingham with Sheffield, Wakefield and Leeds. On 8 June 2017, No. 158784 *Barbara Castle* is seen leaving on a service to Nottingham.

Chesterfield is also the rail destination for occasional charter trains from London, enabling passengers to visit Chatsworth House around 10 miles away. On 6 June 2018, No. 67021 is on the rear of the terminating stock, about to move off to Barrow Hill Sidings for stabling until required for the return working.

The town of Chesterfield was once at the heart of the Yorkshire, Nottinghamshire and Derbyshire coalfield, with a number of collieries in the local area. Today, coal movements by rail through this area are uncommon. On 31 March 2017, GB Railfreight's No. 66709 *Sorrento* heads a rake of empty coal hoppers from Ratcliffe Power Station to their decoy yard at Doncaster.

The downturn in coal traffic led to a number of wagons being surplus to requirements, and operators sought alternative uses for their stock. On 6 August 2017, Colas Rail's No. 70814 heads south on a working from Leeds Stourton to Briton Ferry in South Wales. This rake of former coal wagons is now used on this sand flow.

The coal may have reduced considerably but Chesterfield still has much to offer in the way of alternative freight traffic. In a twenty-four-hour period, on an average weekday, around fifty loco movements is likely, although many run overnight. On 7 August 2019, DB Cargo's No. 60066 heads north on a return working of steel wagons from Wolverhampton Steel Terminal to Immingham.

This freight traffic includes a number of container train workings, including a long-standing working between Leeds Freightliner Terminal and Southampton. The southbound working is seen on 7 August 2019 being hauled by No. 66415 in parent company Genesee & Wyoming's house colours.

Heading in the opposite direction on the same day is GB Railfreight (GBRf)'s No. 66708 *Jayne*. It is on a working from Southampton to the Railport at Doncaster.

Another long-distance working through Chesterfield on 2 August 2019 sees GBRf sister loco No. 66733 *Cambridge PSB* haul a northbound rake of empty gypsum wagons. This was a new contract for GBRf, between Hotchley Hill, in Nottinghamshire, and freight logistics company A. V. Dawson at Middlesbrough, working on behalf of British Gypsum.

GBRf's sole Class 59 loco was in action through Chesterfield on 8 June 2017. Around the time No. 59003 *Yeoman Highlander* had been a regular performer on their working from Bardon Hill in Leicestershire to Tinsley, near Sheffield. It is seen returning south with the rake of empties.

A number of infrastructure trains pass here, operated by various freight companies on behalf of Network Rail. One regular diagram sees a GBRf working between the yards at Doncaster and Toton. On 16 February 2018, No. 66721 *Harry Beck* leads No. 66779 on a working to Toton.

On 1 March 2017, a Direct Rail Services (DRS) infrastructure working heads north with No. 66421 in charge. The wagons had been loaded at Mountsorrel in Leicestershire and were being worked to Carlisle Yard.

Regular freight services through Chesterfield are often complemented by more unusual one-off workings. On 5 June 2015, for instance, DRS Class 68 loco No. 68012 runs south with a short rake of intermodal flat wagons from W. H. Davis at Shirebrook to Derby.

An equally unusual working on 29 January 2019 saw GBRf's No. 66709 *Sorrento* head north with a rake of empty MOD flats. They were en route from MOD Bicester to GBRf's Hexthorpe Yard in Doncaster.

Whitwell to Shirebrook

To the east of Chesterfield, In the far north-east corner of Derbyshire, lie the four stations of Whitwell, Cresswell, Langwith-Whaley Thorns and Shirebrook. These stations were reopened in 1998 when the Robin Hood Line from Nottingham was extended beyond Mansfield to Worksop. On 23 November 2018, No. 158856 waits at Nottingham to leave on an all stations to Worksop service.

The Robin Hood line runs predominantly through the neighbouring county of Nottinghamshire, with just under 6 miles falling within Derbyshire. On 21 March 2014, No. 156498 has just terminated at Worksop and is about to return to Nottingham.

Stations Around Chesterfield

5 miles to the north of Chesterfield is the town of Dronfield. The station originally closed to passengers in 1967. Forty years later, Northern services started calling throughout the day as part of their Nottingham to Leeds service. On 6 February 2019, No. 158784 calls on the 12.15 to Nottingham.

10 miles south of Chesterfield is Alfreton station. When it was reopened in 1973, it was known as Alfreton and Mansfield Parkway, putting the Nottinghamshire town back on the railway map. The reinstatement of a more convenient passenger service through Mansfield itself was not reinstated until twenty-five years later. On 13 April 2018, No. 222101 approaches the station on an EMR empty stock working.

Both Northern and East Midlands Railway (EMR) passenger services call at Alfreton. On 13 April 2018, EMR's No. 158862 calls on a service to Nottingham, where the rear unit will be detached. This leading unit will continue through to Norwich.

To the south of Alfreton, the stations at Langley Mill and Ilkeston have both reopened to passengers in the twenty-first century. Langley Mill reopened in 2008 and the station at Ilkeston was reopened in 2017 on the site of the former Ilkeston Junction station. On 22 June 2018, Northern unit No. 150271 calls on a service from Nottingham to Leeds.

Midland Railway Trust – Butterley and Swanwick Junction

The Midland Railway Trust operates a preserved railway on a 4-mile stretch of the long-closed line from Ambergate to Pye Bridge. Their 0-6-0 'Jinty' steam locomotive, No. 47327, is seen in service, following repaint as S&DJR No. 23.

The Midland Railway is also home to a variety of locos, including 4-6-2 steam locomotive No. 46203 *Princess Margaret Rose*, owned by Princess Royal Class Locomotive Trust.

The Midland Railway has occupied the sites for around fifty years, with the first train running on a section of the line in the early 1980s. The facilities include a museum, with Midland Railway 2-4-0 steam locomotive No. 158A another of the static exhibits.

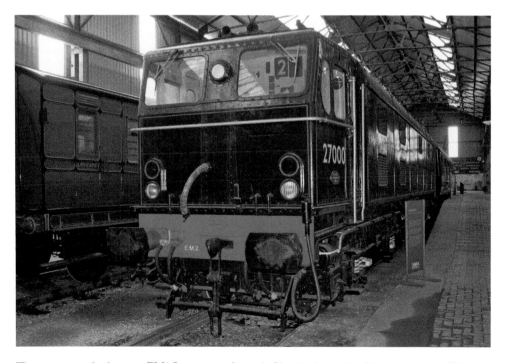

The museum is also home to EM2 Locomotive Society's Class 77 electric loco No. 27000 *Electra*. This 1953 machine was used on express passenger services between Manchester Piccadilly and Sheffield, until the class was withdrawn in 1968.

Several diesel shunters are based here, including No. 08590, which is often used at the yard pilot. The BR blue-liveried shunter carries the name *Red Lion*.

A variety of main line locos can be seen in this line up on 13 September 2013. From right to left, Nos 47761, 31271, D1516 and 45108 are on view.

On the same day, diesel hydraulic loco No. D1048 *Western Lady* was also present. The 'Western' loco had been here since around 1997, and, at the time, was one of seven of the class to survive in preservation.

Several Class 20 locos can be found at the Midland Railway, including No. 20048. This Type 1 diesel loco was seen at Swanwick Junction on 13 September 2013.

Toton

The substantial yards and locomotive depot at Toton are on the county borders of Derbyshire and Nottinghamshire. Since rail privatisation it has been the major UK depot for DB Cargo. A public footpath and bridleway run along the east side of the yard and depot area, complete with a bank offering a good vantage point for rail enthusiasts. This is the view from there on 6 June 2018, with the main depot building in the left of the photo.

A wide variety of liveries are to be seen in this view of the north end of the depot on 17 October 2020. In addition to their own locos, there are several visitors to the DB Cargo depot that day, including GB Railfreight's No. 60026 and DC Rail's No. 60055.

The Toton depot area is the storage location of the majority of out of traffic Class 60 locos. In this view on 28 January 2017, No. 60067 leads a long line of locos stored in the sidings beneath the bank.

To the south of the main Toton depot, in among the vegetation on 17 October 2020, there are more stored Class 60 locos, including Nos 60073, 60008 (still carrying *Sir William McAlpine* nameplate), 60018, 60004 and 60014, all visible in this view.

Back in January 2016, three out-of-use diesel shunters are awaiting a decision on their future. Locos Nos 08676, 08630 and 08802 all carry the EWS livery. In March that year the company was rebranded as DB Cargo UK.

Colas Rail's No. 56094 was stabled on the depot on 31 March 2019. It had arrived at Toton a few days earlier on a light engine move from Barnetby.

Another visitor to Toton was Freightliner's No. 59203, seen on 17 October 2020. The loco had received the livery of its parent company, Genessee & Wyoming, at the paintshops here. It was awaiting its return to Freightliner action.

With the loss of coal traffic in the Toton area, the yards here are used chiefly in connection with Network Rail infrastructure work, particularly at weekends. On Saturday 28 January 2017, No. 66207 is about to reverse on to a rake of wagons. Sister locos Nos 66130, 66031 and 66011 are all awaiting departure on weekend infrastructure work.

It is not just DB Cargo that are involved in these infrastructure duties. On 19 April 2017, Direct Rail Services' No. 66426 is at the head or a rake of wagons awaiting to return to Doncaster.

GB Railfreight's celebrity loco No. 66779 *Evening Star* was another visitor on infrastructure work on 22 July 2019. It is stabled at the head of a rake of side tippler ballast wagons.

A number of other freight workings are scheduled to pass through the yard's centre roads. On 5 October 2016, for example, Freightliner's No. 66604 is seen heading south on a working from Earles Sidings to the cement terminal at Walsall, West Midlands.

It is the view of the locomotives on the depot, however, that brings enthusiasts to the area. This view on 19 April 2017 is typical of the cluster of locomotives usually seen around the north end of the depot. Identifiable in this view are Nos 66144, 66160, 66174, 66022, 66017, 66168 and 60058.

To the west of Toton lies the triangular junction at Trent, with the local stations at Long Eaton and Spondon both situated on the line from there towards Derby. On 1 February 2019, CrossCountry Trains' Class 170 unit No. 170107 calls at Long Eaton on a service to Nottingham.

On the same day, sister CrossCountry unit No. 170116 passes EMR's No. 153374 as both trains call at Long Eaton. The station is halfway between Derby and Nottingham, approximately 8 miles from each.